KU-476-755

THE QUIET GARDEN

SPIRIT OF NATURE

The Quiet
Garden

DAVID BOAG

A LION BOOK

Introduction

'Now the Lord God had planted a garden in the east, in Eden; and there he put the man he had formed. And the Lord God made all kinds of trees grow out of the ground... trees that were pleasing to the eye and good for food.' This story, from the book of Genesis in the Bible, continues to explain how this perfect garden was spoilt by Adam's disobedience to God. Everyone has their own ideas about the perfect garden; perhaps some imagine a formal arrangement of beautiful plants, while others picture a wilderness of wonderful colours and smells. Personally, I enjoy the thought that the animals and birds which inhabited that garden were approachable and unafraid of human beings. Whatever we conjure up in the imagination, often we try to surround ourselves with that perfect environment where God first intended us to live.

Most of us cannot begin to create the perfect garden of our dreams – we are limited by time, money, size and of course effort! But whatever our choice, as we relax on the lawn we are not alone, but are surrounded by wildlife. For many of us the creatures around us go unseen, or at least unnoticed, because many of them are too small, too secretive or nocturnal.

For many people the wild birds and butterflies in the garden give just as much pleasure as the beautiful cultivated flowers. Indeed, some people go to great lengths to encourage birds by providing food and nest boxes, and attract butterflies by growing certain plants which they enjoy. However, there is another side to the wild creatures that share our property which makes them far less popular. An enthusiastic gardener trembles at the thought of caterpillars, moles or bindweed and so the life of a gardener is a constant struggle to maintain the artificial balance that he or she chooses.

Wildlife owned the property long before we did and is slow to give ground to the hand of humans. The best approach is to to discover and

enjoy the variety of wildlife that chooses to live with us. I cannot help feeling most privileged that a spotted flycatcher should come all the way from southern Africa to nest in my porch and that a hedgehog decided the best place to make a nest was in my rubbish tip. Not all wildlife is quite so attractive, nevertheless there is always more to be discovered for those who have the enthusiasm to find it. As we try to design our idyllic gardens perhaps we can spare a little space for those creatures and plants that have no deeds of ownership but were created for us to enjoy.

People can be very fickle when it comes to their own property. Bullfinches are beautiful birds – until they take the buds from the fruit trees; daisies are so pretty – except in the lawn; badgers are wonderful wild animals to have in the garden – unless they dig up the grass. I hope that as you turn the pages of this book you will enjoy the wildlife I have found in a variety of gardens. At times you will be grateful that some of the wildlife is not in *your* garden – or at least you may think it isn't!

The majority of wild creatures that make their way into human habitation are regarded as pests or vermin. Nevertheless, all sorts of different animals choose to share human homes, despite our attitude towards them. In fact some have become so dependent upon our houses that we name them appropriately – house sparrow, house-fly, house martin, house mouse, house spider and so on.

Some animals that are difficult to tolerate indoors are more acceptable in the garden shed. Perhaps some members of the family open the shed door with more caution than others – although it is difficult to imagine what harm a mouse or a spider can cause a grown man or woman!

House mice are inquisitive little rodents that explore every nook and cranny of the garden shed. Their lives seem to be inextricably linked to humans. Only a few years after the last crofter left the remote St Kilda island, house mice became extinct, even though they had shared the island with people for hundreds of years.

Large, hairy house spiders are found in all kinds of buildings as well as houses and a female may live up to four years. When she lays her eggs she wraps them in silk and stands protectively near them. This one has used a roll of old carpet as a nursery.

POND LIFE

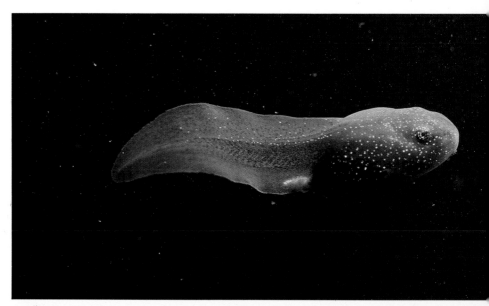

A pond probably doubles the number of species of wild creatures in a garden. Not only does it provide a location where frogs, toads and newts can spawn, it also enables beautiful dragonflies and damselflies to breed. There are less obvious benefits – as birds come to drink and new plants establish themselves around the margins.

A male palmate newt can be distinguished from smooth newts by a fine filament at the end of the tail and by black, webbed hind feet. Newts only visit ponds for the spring and summer breeding season.

LEFT: *At about three weeks old the tadpole of a common frog is still feeding on algae and breathing with internal gills. It takes a total of about twelve weeks for the tadpole to develop into a tiny frog, when it will leave the pond.*

RIGHT: *Even the most unlikely looking ponds can play host to dragonfly larva such as the downy emerald. The larva are rather unattractive predators that remain hidden at the bottom of the water for most of their lives. When one emerges, its old skin breaks open and a miracle of packaging is revealed – a long slender body and large delicate wings expand before your eyes. After a rest the beautiful insect takes to the air as though it had never been restricted to the muddy depths of the pond.*

Wild plants invade the garden at every opportunity. They are regarded as weeds, but if they escape the lawn mower or gardener's hoe for long enough, they will produce flowers. Perhaps they are not as spectacular as the species we cultivate but they have a simple beauty that is natural to the British Isles.

Barely has the soil been freshly dug before wild plants establish themselves. It is an indication of the abundance of seeds carried by the wind or lying dormant in the ground.

10

Viper's bugloss is more likely to be discovered on sea cliffs or sand dunes, than growing on the roadside verge of a modern housing estate.

As every gardener knows, many wild plants try to establish themselves in the bare soil between rows of vegetables. Tiny flowers of scarlet pimpernel race to set seed, establishing the next generation, before they are weeded out.

A tiny crack between a concrete path and the house wall is sufficient room for a smooth sow-thistle to establish itself. Once the petals have fallen, the seed head resembles a miniature dandelion clock.

People long to surround themselves with beauty, and, in the garden, try to make use of plants in a way that is pleasing to the eye.

Different flowers are chosen for all sorts of reasons; they may be native to an area, or simply have lovely bright colours. Brick walls can be screened by shrubs, and climbing plants break up the harsh outline of a garden shed. Many people try to hide the things which they create themselves, by using plants that are part of the natural creation.

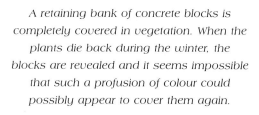

A retaining bank of concrete blocks is completely covered in vegetation. When the plants die back during the winter, the blocks are revealed and it seems impossible that such a profusion of colour could possibly appear to cover them again.

Although red valerian was first introduced as a garden plant, it now grows wild in a great variety of waste places.

13

The Welsh poppy is a native plant found growing wild in the south west of England and in Wales, but it has been cultivated in gardens throughout the country.

Winged visitors arrive in every garden, call on every flower box and visit every plant pot. The most noticeable are butterflies and their night-time counterparts, moths.

In general they are welcomed because of their beauty as well as their work in pollinating flowers. Even so there are exceptions; both the small and large white caterpillars feed on cabbage plants which makes then unpopular (sometimes they are referred to as cabbage whites). The caterpillars of most species feed on wild plants in the hedgerow or wood but the adults, being so mobile, are able to make use of garden flowers.

Some people who enjoy butterflies deliberately grow a selection of flowers that are attractive to them. The highly scented flowers of buddleia can be covered with many different species of butterflies during mid-summer. Moths are equally attracted to its blooms and a visit at night with a torch can be most rewarding.

14

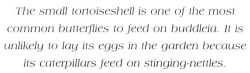

The small tortoiseshell is one of the most common butterflies to feed on buddleia. It is unlikely to lay its eggs in the garden because its caterpillars feed on stinging-nettles.

A rare visitor; a clouded yellow cannot survive British winters at any stage of its life. Indeed, many years may pass without one being seen, but every so often a sudden influx of many thousands arrive from southern France. They decorate the fields, woods and gardens but all of them will die, unable to establish the next generation.

An elephant hawk-moth is resting during the daylight on a windowsill because, like many species of moths, it was attracted to a light from the window during the night. The caterpillar, which feeds on willowherbs, gives the moth its strange name. If disturbed, it draws its head back into its body giving it the appearance of a bulbous elephant head, with two large eyes.

The sight of apples rotting on the ground can seem like a waste, but it is a delightful harvest for several species of birds. Thrushes in particular look for the fruit – redwings and fieldfares fly in from northern Europe to join thrushes; mistle thrush, song thrush and blackbird, in the bonanza of fruit and berries found in the autumn months.

The rotting fruit also provides a meal for less popular creatures in the garden. Wasps and flies buzz around the fruit during the day and slugs take their turn in the hours of darkness. The presence of slugs attracts hedgehogs into the orchard and so the cycle of life continues.

16

Once the sweet, juicy apples of the orchard are finally eaten the thrushes will turn their attention to the wild crab apples that can be found in the hedge.

The blackbird had no hope of defending this supply of apples from the heavier and stronger fieldfare. So it simply waited in a nearby bush and each time the fieldfare dashed off in pursuit of another hopeful bird, the blackbird hopped in and enjoyed a meal.

Large flocks of fieldfares arrive in Britain in autumn from their breeding area in Scandinavia. Although they commonly feed in flocks, where a good supply of food is discovered an individual will stake its claim and defend it against any other birds that would try to steal its plunder.

Two species of mammals found in the garden are hedgehogs and common shrews. They can be referred to as insectivores but their appetite extends to worms, spiders, woodlice, slugs and snails. As a result they are unquestionably a gardener's friend, searching out and eating large numbers of destructive creatures.

The tiny shrew is rarely noticed, partly because of its size but also because of its lightning reflexes. At the slightest sound it disappears from view, unless it is struggling with a large worm or chasing a beetle.

In contrast hedgehogs are often seen ambling about at a leisurely pace after dark. The coat of prickles that is so familiar is an amazing piece of design. A full-grown hedgehog has over 5,000 spines. They are very light but at the same time extremely strong. They can be raised or flattened at will and when a hedgehog rolls into a ball they are very effective protection. Hedgehogs have special muscles that enable them to curl up tightly and they can remain in that position for many hours.

During the night hedgehogs wander from garden to garden and in one night may travel up to 3km (2 miles). It is pleasant to imagine that the hedgehog seen visiting a garden is the same one every night, but tracking has shown that they can be quite nomadic, depending on the time of year.

18

The common shrew has an enormous appetite. It needs to feed about every three hours and consumes almost its own body-weight in food each day. As a result it is active during the day as well as at night – rushing about with frantic urgency as it searches for its next meal.

It has been claimed that the silk produced by a spider to create its web is the strongest known material. Human endeavour has never been able to match its strength, flexibility and lightness. Its unique qualities are well illustrated when a wasp or bee flies at full speed into the sticky threads.

There are over six hundred different species of spiders to be found in the British Isles and many may be discovered in the garden. Not all spiders spin webs, some hunt by stealth and speed on the ground. Others lie camouflaged on flower heads, waiting for a fly or bee to visit. In Britain there are about forty species of orb-web spider that spin the typical spiral web with radiating supports. Many others spin what to us looks like a tangled mass.

20

A beautifully constructed orb-web is a miracle of both design and construction. Dew of early morning highlights each thread and enables us to view the clever snare. The female garden spider rest in the centre where the web is not sticky.

The most common orb-web spider found in the garden is known as the garden spider. It is sometimes referred to as the cross spider due to a white cross that is visible on the female's back. When the web is first spun, non-sticky silk is used. She later replaces the outer spiral with sticky silk. Spiders usually spin their webs under cover of darkness.

21

A spider's web is useless until the sun melts away the frost which decorates and weighs down the web.

Anyone with a passing interest in birds understands the pleasure that can be had from hanging a wire basket of peanuts in the garden. It is remarkable how quickly birds discover this supply of food, and within a few days many different species will have visited the larder. If it placed in view of a window and easy to see, the pecking order of the different species soon becomes apparent.

Hanging peanuts up increases the local bird population artificially as they begin to rely on that source of food. It is important therefore not suddenly to stop feeding them. These four pictures were taken within about thirty minutes as an indication of the numbers and variety of birds to visit the feeder.

The tit family is usually the first to discover the feeder and blue tits are the most abundant. However, a marsh tit is not slow to follow the blue tit's example, and shares the supply of food.

Great tits are the largest of the family but they do not always manage to dominate the smaller tits. Birds do not feel comfortable feeding so close together but when such a good supply of food is available they will just about tolerate each other.

A nuthatch dominates the feeder and doesn't allow any other birds to feed while it is hungry. Other species have to wait their turn, unless a woodpecker appears and then even the nuthatch has to make way.

The tit family has a reputation for being acrobatic, but a greenfinch is determined to get a meal and demonstrates that it is equally able to hang upside-down.

W e may long for wonderful grass lawns, but nature intends there to be more variety than that.

Leave a lawn uncut for only a few weeks and it soon becomes apparent how many other plants are hidden within the grassy sward. However, many people do enjoy the variety that nature intended, as long as they are in control, and so plants such as snowdrops may be encouraged to grow in the lawn.

Due to constant mowing, self-heal has become stunted but within three days of being cut this persistent plant manages to raise a tiny flower head above the grass.

24

Snowdrops raise their heads as if to promise the spring. Perhaps it is for this reason that we enjoy finding them in a lawn.

It is difficult to imagine why some people find daisies unacceptable in a lawn. They provide a carpet of delicate flowers to walk on and never grow very tall, so require less cutting than grass!

M any birds that are considered to be garden birds are truly birds of the woods. They have learned to exploit people by entertaining them in return for a few peanuts or a handful of suet. The antics the tits perform on the bird table reflect their habits in the woods. Being so light and agile they are able to hang upside-down, land on the most slender twigs and investigate every nook and cranny as they search for hidden insects.

Their choice of nest location in the woods is a hole or cavity in a tree. In the garden, the tits are the most likely birds to make use of a nest box.

The coal tit can be distinguished from other members of the family, not only because it is the smallest, but also by the white patch on the back of its head. It is associated with conifers more than many other birds, and searches the cones for seeds or hidden insects.

The willow tit and marsh tit are difficult to tell apart, but the marsh tit is more attracted to gardens. During the winter it feeds in company with other small birds and a mixed flock of tits, tree creepers and finches often arrive together in the garden.

Several species of finch visit the garden, especially where food is put out to attract them. They are avid seed eaters, and so a good mixture of seed on a bird table is bound to encourage at least a couple of species.

The finch family defies the comments that most British birds are dull, brown and uninteresting. However, in the past their attractive plumage led to them being trapped in large numbers, to be kept as cage birds. This is now illegal in Britain even through they are still captured in other parts of Europe.

The attractive plumage of the goldfinch, with its gold wing-bar and bright red face, make this species easy to identify. The beak is more pointed than other finches because it is designed to extract seeds from thistles, teasels, dandelions and so on.

The chaffinch is possibly the most common bird in Britain, and must visit nearly every garden. It is only the male that is so brightly coloured. Although the female markings are similar, she lacks the pink under-parts and blue-grey head.

LEFT: The beak of a greenfinch is short and strong, designed to deal with larger seeds and in the garden it is particularly fond of sunflower seeds. During the winter, especially during hard weather, they flock together, travelling, feeding and roosting as a group.

BELOW: Even during the spring, when the male is looking at his finest, the female greenfinch does not have his immaculate green and yellow plumage. However, her rather dull green/brown feathers serve a different purpose, providing camouflage when she incubates the eggs.

O f all the birds found in the garden the blackbird and robin must be the species most readily identified. However, the female blackbird sometimes causes confusion as it is not black but dark brown above and rufous-brown below with dark mottlings, and looks more like the other members of the thrush family. Male and female robins are indistinguishable, except presumably to other robins! In many situations both species have become familiar friends in the garden, feeding on a wide variety of insects and berries as well as birdtable scraps.

During winter, blackbirds often raid the pyracantha bushes to feed on the bright berries. A bush can be stripped bare in only a few days and many people grow a variety of shrubs in the garden which produce a good crop of berries each year, especially for the birds to feed on.

Robins find the garden habitat very much
to their liking. Shrubs provide cover and
trees are ideal song perches. The short,
cropped grass of lawns is perfect hunting
places for insects and sheds or bushes
make good nest locations. To a robin, a
house is part of the natural environment, a
place to use rather than avoid.

Nature's activity during the night is revealed in the light of morning. It seems as a silent intruder has crept stealthily into the garden and dusted every possible place with a coating of ice crystals. The results can be breathtaking, transforming even the most mundane objects into fairyland splendour.

Nature seems to agree that a wire mesh fence is most unattractive, so to improve its appearance covers it with sparkling frost.

The snare of a spider is temporarily rendered useless by the frost that clings to each thread.

Each leaf of ivy is rimmed by frost, a familiar plant transformed by a well-known natural phenomenon. Moisture in the air is caught on the leaves and frozen into place creating an overnight miracle.

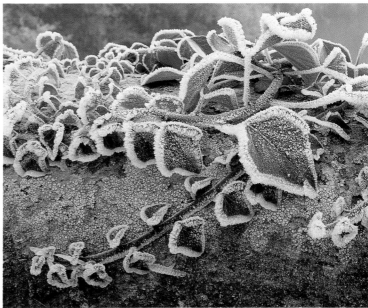

Many different types of fungi may appear in the garden and sometimes they turn up in most unexpected places. Due to the fact that there are so many different species that closely resemble each other, the precise species is often difficult to identify, even for an expert.

It is the fruiting body of fungi that we see; the mycelia, which is the vegetative stage, is usually hidden within the substrate on which it feeds. Many fungi produce their fruiting bodies during the autumn and although some may last only a few hours, others last for months.

Growing out of a gatepost, the leathery brackets of a many-zoned polypore indicate unseen activity within the wood. This species is very common and can be a variety of different colours.

RIGHT: A massive group of honey fungus has developed on an old tree stump. However, this fungus will also attack a living tree and will eventually cause its death. It is a very common species that is more often found in woodland.

BELOW: Overnight, from a lawn, a group of tall fungi appear. Seen at this stage the reason for the name of lawyer's wig is apparent. Within a few hours the caps will open more and, as they deliquesce, black liquid drips to the ground and this gives rise to another common name of shaggy ink cap.

Urban foxes are on the increase, and have now found their way into the heart of many cities. Squirrels have also become a familiar feature of thousands of parks and gardens. In many places squirrels will even take peanuts from human hands, and foxes will eat scraps of food only a few metres from the back door. It is remarkable that they have become so tame considering how cautious, even fearful, their country cousins are.

Human attitudes towards these wild intruders vary from one household to another, but it seems easier to encourage them than it is to prevent them. They are able to negotiate the highest fence, avoid the dog and squeeze through the smallest gap. Perhaps the best advice is 'if you can't beat them join them', and enjoy the privilege of sharing property with free-living animals.

In urban areas red foxes may raise their cubs in the most unlikely locations, including cellars, under sheds or in churchyards. The sight of a family of foxcubs tumbling over each other as they play on the lawn is surely sufficient reward for the small amount of inconvenience they may cause.

Oddly enough the people that most dislike squirrels are those that are interested in wildlife. Peanuts that have been hung up for birds are soon discovered by this inquisitive and agile rodent and so it is dubbed a pest.

Towards the end of winter frogs and toads begin to arrive at the garden pond. The skin colour of the common frog may vary, depending on the soil colour and surrounding vegetation. This enables the frog to remain camouflaged in different habitats. Usually they are a dull green, but bright yellow ones may be found and in some areas they are almost red. However, they remain easily distinguishable from common toads which are usually a dull brown colour. Toads are squat and dumpy creatures with shorter legs and less protruding eyes than frogs and their skin is warty. By comparison the skin of the frog is smooth and it is more agile, hopping rather than crawling like a toad.

38

Common frogs first appear in the garden pond during February or early March. They immediately pair off and as the female lays her eggs in the water the male fertilizes them. Once the breeding season is over they no longer have any interest in the pond unless the weather is exceptionally dry, when they may return to moisten their skin.

Once tadpoles have developed into froglets, they usually leave the pond under cover of darkness. No larger than a fingernail, they soon disappear in the vegetation and so are rarely noticed.

During May, common toads leave the pond having completed breeding and for the rest of the year they are land based. During the day they remain hidden in secret locations beneath stones, amongst roots or under garden sheds.

Acrobatic, agile and attractive, blue tits are visitors to most gardens. During the winter they are only visitors, and the handful that seem to live in one garden are made up of many birds that are passing through on a feeding expedition. By ringing birds it has been shown that hundreds, perhaps even over a thousand, may visit a garden feeder over the period of a winter.

This nomadic life-style comes to an end with the arrival of the breeding season. The travelling party of birds separate into pairs, usually with one bird that is eighteen months old and therefore in its second breeding season, while the other is only six months old and breeding for the first time. Once the eggs are laid in a carefully selected cavity they can no longer move long distances and remain foraging amongst the trees and bushes within a few hundred metres of the nest.

Usually blue tits are the first birds to discover peanuts or hanging suet but they will also take a variety of seeds from a feeder, especially sunflower seeds.

The moment has arrived for the chicks to leave the nest box. It is over the next few days that many are killed by predators and in the garden cats take the greatest toll. Although there may be as many as ten, probably only one of the brood will survive to adult life.

Nest boxes in the garden make ideal nest locations for blue tits, providing security for the growing young. If the nest box is near a window, the activity of the pair can be watched from only a few metres away.

Many creatures that live in the garden escape human attention for most of the time. They lie hidden from view in secret places until the cool of the night, creeping out under cover of darkness.

The nocturnal habits of some creatures are due to their vulnerability to predators. Slow moving slugs, snails and earthworms are unlikely to be taken by birds when it is dark. They are also prone to loosing moisture in the heat of the sun which is an added reason for their nocturnal habits. The toad also has to be careful to keep its skin moist because it absorbs oxygen through its skin to supplement its rather inadequate lungs. But the toad has also discovered that the slugs and worms that are its main source of food are active at night and so the web of life continues through the hours of darkness.

The nocturnal ramble of the toad may take it all over the garden. Moving at a steady crawl it makes its way over a brick path and onto the lawn beyond, where it hopes to discover a few earthworms. At dawn it will return to its safe lair beneath a log pile.

White-lipped banded
snails come in a
huge variety of
colours and
patterns. Their
shells can be bright
yellow, dull brown
or orange and often
they have dark
bands which spiral
to the centre. During
the night they graze
on the leaves of
many garden plants
and are particularly
abundant in areas
of lime-rich soil.

Anyone who has a vegetable plot knows about pigeons! The wood pigeon in particular causes an estimated one million pounds of damage each year to agricultural crops as well as frustrating the efforts of thousands of gardeners. Not only does it eat seeds, grain and nuts, but it also feeds on green leaves of many different crops both in the field and the garden. Pigeons have been persecuted over many years, so it is surprising that they are still so numerous.

It is also strange that the rock dove, descendant of a close relative of such a despised bird, should be treated as a semi-domesticated pet. Even feral pigeon numbers are at pest proportions in many cities where their droppings cause damage to the buildings that replace the natural cliffs of their ancestors.

A more recent invader is the collared dove which illustrates the remarkable adaptability of this family. In the 1930s the collared dove's range was limited to Turkey and the Balkans. By the mid-1950s it had colonized most of Europe and the first bird crossed the sea to England where it was greeted as a real rarity. Today it is so prolific that in some areas this species too is regarded as a pest. It is one of the most remarkable achievements of any bird.

44

Many birds enjoy bathing, and feral pigeons are no exception. A shallow part of a garden pond is a favourite place and is used most days by several birds.

Collared doves are billing and cooing in preparation for the breeding season. The pigeon family has complicated rituals to establish pairs and the bonding activity continues right through the season.

LEFT: In the town garden, wood pigeons can be remarkably tame when compared to the same species in the country.

Even the small things in nature are fascinating, it's just that we need to look closer to enjoy them. The excitement and drama of the great African plains are duplicated in miniature within the garden; the grazing herds, the fearsome predators and the carrion eaters can all be discovered, often in quite surprising ways. Teeming hordes of creatures feed on the plant life, from greenfly to caterpillars – while ladybirds feed on greenfly, wasps take the caterpillars. Centipedes hunt their continent of the garden as effectively as lions hunt the Serengeti plain and woodlice join other creatures mopping up the results of death and decay. To an insect even the orderly garden is a jungle.

46

BELOW: A common green shieldbug scrambles from one honeysuckle leaf to the next. Shieldbugs have needle-like mouth-parts with which they pierce leaves to suck the sap.

One of the largest of British caterpillars, the privet hawk-moth is often found in gardens due to its liking for privet hedges and lilac, but here it is feeding on an ash tree.

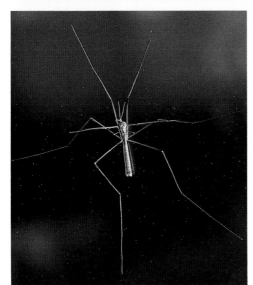

ABOVE: *Although adult wasps enjoy nectar and sweet fruit, they feed their young on meat in the form of insect larvae.*

ABOVE: *Woodlice are found in all rubbish heaps and log piles. Their task in the natural world is to eat dead vegetation and, in doing so, to return nutrients to the soil.*

LEFT: *Seven-spot ladybirds are not often thought of as predators, but they are in fact beetles that hunt and eat greenfly.*

ABOVE: *A crane fly is often referred to as a daddy long-legs. They are attracted to the light of a window and in the morning are found still clinging to the glass.*

More people seem to get excited about a great spotted woodpecker arriving at the bird table than many other species of bird. Unlike the other woodpeckers it comes readily to food; peanuts, suet and even sunflower seeds are popular. It is often confused with the lesser spotted woodpecker but there is no need for confusion because the lesser is only the size of a sparrow and has a boldly barred back rather than large white shoulder patches. The great spotted is much larger, closer in size to a blackbird or starling, and has a red patch under the tail.

Sometimes the greater spotted woodpecker appears to be eating a huge quantity of food, visiting the bird table every few minutes and flying off with its beak crammed full. It is probable that it is storing nuts for use later in winter. Many birds behave in this way because they are unaware that the supply will continue and instinctively make use of the apparent glut of food. Nuts and seeds may be hidden in nooks and crannies in a tree or buried amongst roots or leaf litter. As a result of this method of seed dispersal a sunflower may begin to grow in the garden in a most unexpected place.

Both the green woodpecker and lesser spotted woodpecker may visit the garden but neither of them has learned to exploit the bird table.

To prevent woodpeckers and other birds flying off with vast quantities of food most people put peanuts in a holder of wire mesh. This means that the birds can only get small fragments out at a time. If a woodpecker arrives, all other birds stand aside, having to wait until the woodpecker has left before they can resume feeding.

The bird table is empty and one might imagine that the great spotted woodpecker is looking into the window hoping to attract the attention of the occupants. However, they tend to be shy birds and often beat a fast retreat at the sight of a human, even where they regularly feed in gardens.

The male great spotted woodpecker has a bright red patch on the back of its head, but the female does not. The juvenile birds have red crowns, as if they were wearing red caps.

Many flowers of the wild have been introduced into gardens and while some have been cultivated out of all recognition, others remain as nature intended them to be. Some of these plants, such as primroses, remain a common sight in the woods, hedges and banks. Others, such as the fritillary or snake's head, have become rare in the wild and the garden is their last haven. Surprisingly, many wild plants are difficult to grow from seed in cultivated situations but it is illegal to dig up wild specimens.

Many people recognize primroses as a symbol of spring. Once established they may form large clumps and seem able to thrive in almost every location, even on the edge of a path.

Wild cowslips were once so popular that they were picked in huge bunches until they became an uncommon sight. Recently they have made a comeback.

50

Where the fritillary plant grows in the
wild it is found in the short grass of
meadows. It follows that in the garden it
thrives best in areas of uncut lawn. It
grows from bulbs and when
left undisturbed this beautiful flower may
form quite large colonies.

Both song thrushes and mistle thrushes make use of gardens, where they are particularly fond of searching lawns early in the morning for earthworms. The two species are often confused but the mistle thrush is slightly larger and has a more grey/brown appearance. By comparison the smaller song thrush seems more rounded, less angular, and is a warm brown colour. The spots on the chest of mistle thrushes are bolder and more rounded but this is hard to determine unless the two species are seen together.

Both of these species are splendid songsters and sing throughout the winter and on to the end of spring. They select high branches in trees or rooftops as suitable song perches, and their song is full of rich, fluty notes that declare their territory.

52

One of the earliest nests to be found in the garden are those of the mistle thrush. They are usually placed several metres high in the fork of a tree and often appear quite exposed. On other occasions they may be more hidden by ivy and although it is the female that does most of the incubation, both the parents feed the growing chicks.

Song thrushes hide their nests in a variety of locations. Sometimes they make use of garden sheds, but usually they are placed in more natural locations. Thick shrubs, especially evergreens such as holly, are favourite along with ivy covered trees or walls. The completed nest has a smooth lining of rotten wood or mud and its eggs, which are bright blue, are very attractive.

53

Autumn arrives in the garden in the same way as the woods. As the leaves on the deciduous trees change colour to the tints of autumn, nuts, berries and other fruits ripen. The harvest of natural fruits is enormous; most of it is of little value to humans but is designed for the wild creatures that visit the garden. The importance of nature's harvest is well illustrated by the squirrels' industry in the autumn. They urgently gather nuts and acorns, carrying them off to bury them for use later in the winter. Without this hidden supply of food many squirrels would die.

In a good year an oak tree can produce thousands of acorns, whilst in other years hardly any at all. Out of all the acorns that fall to the ground very few will even germinate. Most will be eaten by jays, squirrels and other animals.

54

Many people recognize conkers as a result of children's games that they used to play. Hidden within a tough, spiky casing, the large seeds are well protected until the case splits open, releasing them to the ground. Although the horse chestnut is an introduced species it has become very much part of the British countryside.

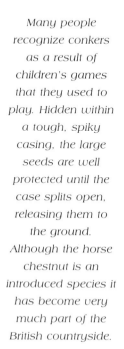

*Full grown holly trees may reach a
height of fifteen metres, but few people
allow them to grow so large in the garden
because little can grow beneath a holly's
shade. The prickly, evergreen leaves and
bright red berries make it one of the most
attractive British plants.*

Badgers hold a fascination for many people, their nocturnal habits and shy natures making them difficult to observe. However, if a sett is in the vicinity, they regularly visit gardens, digging under fences to make an entrance.

Badgers can be encouraged into the garden by providing a regular supply of food and they will take all sorts of household scraps from bread to bananas, meat to milk. They will even become accustomed to feeding in artificial light, coming right up to the back door. But before encouraging them one needs to be aware that they are wild animals that may dig up the lawn or root about the vegetable plots in search of earthworms.

Trotting along the garden path a badger keeps its nose to the ground scenting for earthworms, beetles, slugs and so on that have strayed onto the path. The badger's sense of smell is well developed – something humans find difficult to understand, having such a poor sense of smell.

A bucket left out overnight is inspected by a badger, which is hoping to find something edible inside. Although a badger is inquisitive, strange objects left on the lawn are treated with suspicion. Its sensitive nose sniffs for any sign of danger before it feels confident enough to approach.

Two species of of native plants that are often found in gardens are wild strawberry and lily of the valley. They both originate from woodland habitats but seem just as at home in the garden. Indeed, lily of the valley used to be common in woodland throughout the country but today it is more frequently seen in gardens. Its fragrant scent hides the fact that all parts of the plant contain a deadly poison.

By comparison, the fruit of the wild strawberry is good to eat although not as sweet as cultivated species.

Lily of the valley is best seen in flower during May when the delicate white flowers hang trembling on long spikes.

LEFT: Although lily of the valley produces seed it more commonly multiplies by sending up new shoots from its creeping underground stems. The result is a dense patch that slowly spreads outwards.

RIGHT: There can be little confusion about the fruit of a wild strawberry plant; it is a miniature replica of the cultivated strawberry.

Pushing its way through a crack in the concrete a wild strawberry plant has taken root. They spread readily from seed as well as runners and so this little reminder of the woods may pop up anywhere in the garden.

A delightful addition to summer flowers are the butterflies that feed upon them. Indeed, they could be described as flying flowers, but they hold an added interest because they are so unpredictable. One can never be certain which species may turn up next or where they may choose to settle.

Butterflies go through four major stages in their life cycle. First the egg (ovum) is laid and then a caterpillar (larva) appears. The next stage is as a chrysalis (pupa), until finally the adult flying insect emerges (imago). Each stage is totally different, bearing no resemblance to another. Even the food plants of the caterpillar and adults are completely different. It is one of creation's most remarkable inventions that we have grown to accept and perhaps no longer appreciate.

A painted lady butterfly settles on a paving slab for a few minutes, spreading its wings to gather the warmth of the sun.

Brimstone butterflies hibernate in adult form. As a result they are among the first butterflies to appear in the garden in spring.

LEFT: *Winged, adult red admiral butterflies enjoy feeding on buddleia but they will lay their eggs on nettles, which is the caterpillar's food plant.*

Many species of birds make use of buildings as places to nest. They manage to find little hiding places in all sorts of locations. Some enter sheds and outbuildings, others find an entrance into the loft space, chimney pots, holes in a wall, in the porch, under the eaves – the choices seem endless.

It is frustrating how often we are unaware of the nest until the youngsters have grown up and fledged. It illustrates how secretive some birds are about their nest location. For example, a robin that gathers worms from a metre away as someone digs the garden will not take them to its nest if a human in sight, preferring to wait even though its beak is crammed to capacity.

Equally remarkable is that many species of birds that are wary of human activity in the countryside choose to associate with human habitation to nest.

The domed nest of this wren was situated in the rafters of a garden shed. The male made the main structure out of grass, moss, leaves and even a bit of string. The female then lined it with lots of feathers.

A hole in the wall of an out-building was perfectly suited for a robin's nest. It was partly filled with dead leaves and moss and then the hollow was lined with fine grass and hair, ready to receive the eggs.

A mountain of twigs have been carried into the loft space by jackdaws, far more than was needed to construct the nest. The young birds hear the parents arrive by the sound their feet make as they land on the tiles above and the chicks respond by eagerly calling.

A well-established herbaceous border often produces surprises for those who are interested in natural history. Many of the plants found there originate from the surrounding countryside. Some have remained as nature first created them, whilst others have been cultivated into new varieties.

One of the best examples are foxgloves. They are abundant in the woods where even the occasional white one appears as an oddity. In the garden humans tend to concentrate on the oddities, encouraging different colour forms. As a result not only are the natural rich purple types found in the garden but a whole range of paler pinks, right through to white.

64

Yellow iris, also called yellow flag, is common along rivers, streams and ditches. It makes a beautiful flowering plant for the garden, especially in damp areas of soil.

Columbine is now more often found in gardens than in the woods where it originated. The natural colour is deep violet but in gardens, pink or even white varieties may be found.

Jacob's ladder, honeysuckle, foxgloves, delphiniums, lupins and irises are all jumbled together to create a riot of colour. A mixture of wild and cultivated plants in a delightful herbaceous border.

WEEDS!

If I dared to suggest that there are no such things as weeds I am sure every gardener would be incensed. The dictionary describes a weed as being 'a wild plant growing where it is not wanted', so on that basis I have to agree that there are weeds. I simply prefer to call them wild plants!

By calling them weeds we tend to ignore or dislike them, yet they are all part of natural creation and if viewed through the eyes of a naturalist can be beautiful and interesting.

Everyone has their own opinions, and it is a quirk of human nature that a plant weeded out by one person is encouraged by the next.

Hedge bindweed is a tenacious, creeping and climbing perennial that is the bane of many gardeners' lives. Even so, cultivated versions are available where the white trumpet-shape flowers are replaced by flowers of vibrant blue.

Forget-me-not outgrew its welcome and became too abundant in the flower border. At that stage it changed from a pleasing herb to a weed.

Exotic clematis and wild forget-me-not have been brought together in the garden, but would never meet in nature. The large, showy flowers of clematis seem to exaggerate the tiny simplicity of the natural forget-me-nots.

In general, daisies in the lawn are unacceptable. However, there can be few lawns where they have not established themselves, illustrating the tenacity of this wild plant.

The variety of birds that can be attracted into the garden is astonishing. A handful of mixed bird seed, or a few peanuts is all that is needed, provided the table is kept supplied every day.

Some birds that are reluctant to come to a bird table feed avidly on seed spilt on the lawn, whilst other species only seem interested in peanuts suspended in mid-air. Birds that are unseen in one garden may be common at another feeder only a few miles away.

Along with the common chaffinches, greenfinches, sparrows, tits, and so on, more unusual species also turn up and can become regular visitors to the garden.

As its name suggests the reed bunting is a bird associated with the riverbank. But where a garden is not too far from reeds, they have learned to exploit the easy supply of food from a seed feeder.

Bullfinches regularly visit gardens with fruit trees to steal the buds in early spring but otherwise they are not thought of as garden birds. However, for the whole of one winter a pair visited the same garden several times a day to feed on black sunflower seeds.

68

Although a common species on farmland, yellowhammers are not thought of as garden birds. However, in this location a flock of over a dozen were in and out of the garden for most of the winter, feeding on grain.

Siskins are woodland birds feeding on alder, spruce and pine seeds. In recent years they have become increasingly common in gardens, especially in hard winters, when they are especially fond of peanuts.

Concrete and steel seem unlikely companions for wild birds and mammals but plainly they do not find man-made objects too offensive. Wild animals need only a few things to make a location suitable for their requirements. A good supply of food is essential as well as a suitable place to nest and raise their young. A safe retreat is also important to many creatures and most birds appreciate a suitable song perch. These simple requirements are not difficult to find even in the heart of a city, and wildlife is quick to exploit every possibility.

Out of all birds, starlings have learned to make use of a man-made habitat to perfection. Although they most enjoy searching for insects in short turf found in parks and lawns, they also readily feed on a variety of edible scraps discarded by humans.

A territorial bird, this pied wagtail was attracted to the car mirror. It assumed that its reflection was an intruder, and battled with this enemy. (If it happens, cover the mirror – it saves the wagtail's nerves, and a mess on the window!)

Crouched on a garden patio, a grey squirrel nibbles a tasty morsel. Provided the garden has a few tall trees as a safe retreat squirrels in a town are perfectly content to share their lives with people. However, by comparison their country cousins are extremely wary of human activity.

Spotted flycatchers specialize in catching insects on the wing. They watch every movement from look-out perches, which may include an iron fence or a branch of a tree – both are equally suitable. Flicking into the air they snatch passing insects with acrobatic ease, returning to the look-out post only a second later.

Few people spend very much time watching sparrows, probably because they are seen as small, brown, common birds. But it doesn't mean that they aren't interesting.

House sparrows are cheeky little characters that choose to live in close proximity to people. They are equally satisfied feeding on bread crusts thrown onto a lawn as foraging grain from a farm. Very few house sparrows nest in what might be considered natural locations. Rather they choose cavities in buildings, squeezing under the eaves of a house or amongst the rafters of an outbuilding.

Although a dunnock is also small, brown and about the same size as a sparrow it is not related, despite its other common name of hedge sparrow. It is unlikely to join other birds on a bird table, preferring to remain on the ground picking up fallen crumbs.

Dunnocks are territorial birds so large flocks are never found. This is because they are insectivorous and so every morsel has to be searched for and there is never the large supply that sparrows enjoy. Everything in nature has a reason!

The markings of the male house sparrow are not apparent when the bird is first fledged and all the juveniles look alike. But in August or September when they moult, the sexes can easily be distinguished.

The female house sparrow does not have the distinctive markings of the male but she retains her strong character. Sparrows have a powerful instinct to form flocks, which has its advantage when an abundant supply of food is discovered. However, this also causes fights over the most tasty scraps.

Many years ago favourite plants were gathered from the wild and brought home to brighten gardens. As a result, plants that reflect a variety of different wild habitats can be discovered even within a small garden.

The violet/blue flowers of the lesser periwinkle brings a flavour of hedgerow and woodland into the garden.

When broom is in
full flower the
vibrant splashes of
yellow are
reminiscent of a cliff-
top walk or a stroll
on a heath.

A clump of bell
heather reflects
something of the
splendid dry heath
or moorland
habitat.

Bird-baths can be purchased in dozens of different shapes and sizes and ornament countless gardens. Some are used constantly whilst others may be completely ignored. The frustrating thing is that there seems to be no way of ensuring their success.

Birds seem to have their own secret criteria and defy human logic with their behaviour. Although surrounded with bird-baths of just the right shape and size, with each placed in exactly the correct position, the birds completely ignore them and chose an old frying pan. I have never known a frying pan like it! Hardly a moment of the day passed without a visitor arriving, either for a quick drink or a full wash and brush up. I estimated that on one summer's day over two hundred and fifty visits were made to the frying pan and at least ten different species were involved. Interestingly, some species, such as the dunnock, came within a few centimetres but never drank or bathed.

The great spotted woodpecker took all the amenities that the frying pan offered. Each time it spent a long while drinking before leaping in and fluttering with such vigour that water flew in all directions.

House sparrows were regular visitors to the frying pan, but they did not usually stay long unless two or three came together. The company encouraged them to throw caution to the wind and hop into the shallow water where they splashed about with such abandon that their feathers became quite sodden.

Although greenfinches enjoy bathing it seems they prefer not to use frying pans! Certainly they regularly took sips of water, gulping it down with upturned heads, but I never saw one jump in.

The changing seasons are as much part of the garden as they are part of the woods. The natural progression of seasons follow year after year. In fact they are so reliable that we often stop enthusing about the arrival of spring or the colours of autumn as it has become commonplace to us.

The months of spring push aside the long winter and as the day length increases and ground temperatures warm, new life appears. Buds on the trees, blossom, early flowers, birds singing, early butterflies – nature is on the move again.

Blossom on the pear tree not only provides food for pollinating insects, it also offers hope of a good crop in the autumn.

78

Lifting their showy heads towards the blue sky, cultivated daffodils are found in almost every garden.

The delicate blossom of blackthorn contrasts with the hard dark spines that give the shrub its name.

Each season has its own beauty but it is sometimes difficult to see during a period of endless wind-blown drizzle. Eventually even winter produces its reward for our tolerance, its foul mood having passed for a while.

Every leaf, twig and branch is decorated by an overnight frost and the garden is enveloped with patterns of ice crystals that no human artists could create.

It was the morning of Christmas Eve when these photographs were taken and the sparkle of the frost seemed to exaggerate the excitement of the season.

A mosaic of twigs and ice crystals lifted up to a clear blue sky.

Nature seems able to achieve the impossible when it comes to creating patterns.

A fir tree is decorated by nature in readiness for Christmas Day.

Winter is a difficult time for many wild animals and each species has its own method of overcoming the problems. Some hide away little stores of food, while others use fat reserves put on in the summer and autumn. It is often thought that an easy way for animals to solve the problem is to hibernate and escape the rigours of winter by having a long, deep sleep. However, hibernation is not that simple and I have come to think of it as being closer to death than to sleep. Although this is not technically correct it throws a different light on hibernation.

During hibernation the creatures' hearts only beat once in a while and breathing almost stops. The animals' body temperature drops so low it almost matches the surrounding frosty countryside and feels cold to touch; that is more than just sleep. In fact many animals that hibernate never wake up again and slip over the edge into death. Hibernation is not an easy option. It is a difficult process; only a few British mammals truly hibernate. Hedgehogs, dormice and bats complete the list.

82

Hedgehogs only hibernate for about three or four months and even then they may wake up on mild evenings taking a stroll to search for food, before returning to hibernate once more.

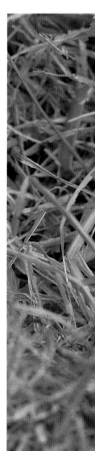

Having been out of hibernation for several weeks, a brown long-eared bat, for some unknown reason, did not return to its roost. It remained hung up all day on the garden shed, flying again at dusk.

A common dormouse found a bag of straw that had been left in the corner of a shed. Curling up into a tight ball, it remained as if dead for almost six months.

You can never be certain who visits the garden during the hours of darkness. Once the curtains are drawn and the lights switched off, more takes place in the garden than many imagine.

Some mammals of the night are visitors from the surrounding countryside, while others are residents who lie asleep all day in hidden burrows. Many gardens are linked together by animal highways that may run from a hole in the fence, through a broken gate and into a gap under a shed.

A night-time vigil watching the bird table yields some surprising results. Food that is spilt on the ground attracts mice, voles, and even rats, and some rats have taught themselves how to climb up onto the table to enjoy a feast.

The activity and scent of small rodents attracts a weasel to investigate a log pile. It has taken a detour from a hunting foray in the nearby woods, into the garden.

84

A bank vole creeps out of its daytime hideaway as darkness covers the garden. It is not entirely nocturnal but during the day it is much more secretive, keeping to hidden runs and burrows.

Common rats have their regular routes through gardens and know exactly where every hole can be found in a fence. They are social animals that live in colonies and although not popular in the garden they actually do little damage.

Rockeries demonstrate how people endeavour to recreate a natural habitat within a garden. The desire may be only sub-conscious, but nevertheless rockeries are a reminder of wild areas of mountain or coast. Many plants that are grown on a rockery originate from those wild locations and both alpine plants as well as coastal species are represented.

To animal species that visit the garden, a rockery may provide a safe haven where they can hide beneath the low growing plants. Birds may use the higher boulders as vantage points to watch the garden, whilst butterflies enjoy basking on the warm rocks. Ant nests and other small invertebrates are often to be found hidden beneath the heavy stones.

A resident robin regularly perches on the rockery watching the lawn for any sign of food – or cats!

86

Wall butterflies are particularly fond of sun bathing and a rockery boulder provides a perfect sun-trap.

A slow-worm slips out from under a low-growing conifer to bathe in the sunshine, absorbing the warmth from the rock as well as direct from the sun.

Holes and cavities in the garden are often in short supply and birds that use this type of location to nest sometimes have to leave the garden to find suitable sites. Old fruit trees in particular are prone to rotting and provide excellent hollows, but often old trees are removed from the garden to make way for new ones.

One particular hole was used by blue tits for two years but as the hole became larger a great tit took occupation. Over the following few years sparrows raised their young in the hollow before starlings took over ownership. The starlings stayed for six years, although on one occasion a pair of nuthatches attempted a take-over. Eventually little owls moved in but their first attempts were thwarted by jackdaws; however, the second year they successfully raised a brood.

So much activity over one hole, in a tree that many of us would have felled years ago.

88

Cavity nest locations are secure places to raise young. Starling chicks remain in the nest until three weeks old and are well developed when they fledge.

An adult starling searches for food on the lawn to feed to its growing brood.

Little owls make use of hollow trees as nest locations and are often found in orchards. They hunt during twilight hours for many species of insects and rodents that are regarded as pests.

Depending on where a garden is situated, almost any kind of woodland or hedgerow bird can find a suitable corner to nest.

It is possible to identify many nests simply by where they are located and how they are constructed. For example, the warblers tend to make their nests using dead grasses, most finches include moss, and thrushes incorporate mud or rotten wood. A song thrush nest is well hidden within two metres of the ground, compared to the mistle thrush's, which is usually much higher and often seems quite exposed.

The construction of a nest is another illustration of the miracle of instinct. Each bird knows how and where to make its nest without any instruction or example.

The nest of a chaffinch is very neat and compact; it looks too small to contain a growing brood of four or five chicks.

90

Spotted flycatchers regularly use buildings as a location for their nests. Often they may be situated against a wall, on a rafter, or in little cavities. Open nest boxes are regularly used.

Fruit trees in a garden often provide nest sites for goldfinches although they will use other locations. They are well camouflaged and hidden by leaves. However, many eggs and chicks are still lost to predators such as squirrels, magpies and cats.

Made from a tangle of dry grass stems and dead leaves a chiffchaff places its nest only just above the ground. It is a loosely domed structure with a side entrance hole, and rapidly becomes hidden as vegetation grows up around it.

Swallows and house martins so often use buildings that it is difficult to imagine how they survived before humans provided them with nesting places. Originally they would have used rock faces and caves but very few use these natural locations today.

   Both of these species are well known as migrants and their arrival has come to symbolize the start of summer. Over-wintering in southern Africa, they travel north to make use of the longer summer days to feed on insects which they catch on the wing. In a good season a pair may raise two or even three broods, each with four or five young. However, the long migration the young birds have to undertake results in a high mortality rate.

Swallows prefer to enter a building to construct their nests, and they will even fly into an open kitchen or bedroom window looking for a suitable place. In general they select rafters in a shed or out-building but this may be disastrous if the entrance window or door is then closed.

House martins construct their nests on the outside of buildings just under the eaves. They are cleverly made from balls of mud collected from a muddy puddle or riverbank. The mud is plastered onto the wall until it forms a bowl with an opening at the top. House martins tend to nest in colonies, and many nests may be situated close to each other under the eaves of a house.

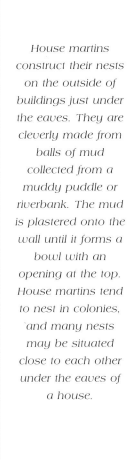

Towards the end of summer, hundreds of house martins gathered. Most of the time they were sitting on telephone wires or hawking the sky. Suddenly they landed on a roof, fluffed out their feathers and preened or sunbathed.

Index to Photographs

94

Acknowledgments

It all began as I sat across a desk from Rebecca Winter at Lion Publishing. I had suggested the idea of producing a book as a celebration of God's creation, and I proposed several chapters. Rebecca shared my enthusiasm and we agreed on a completion date. I was then taken by surprise when Rebecca asked if, rather than just one, I would photograph and write a set of four books, each covering a different environment. This was even more exciting than I had imagined and I eagerly agreed. However, the completion date remained unchanged! So began the most hectic and challenging two years of my life.

As I drove home, I worked out that I had about five hundred working days to photograph five hundred wildlife subjects, and to write text and captions. The four environments I selected were coast, woodland, river and garden, and during the following two years I travelled from the most northern tip of Scotland to Welsh islands, and from the east coast to the south-west tip of England.

The photographic equipment I used included two single lens reflex camera bodies and four lenses — 28mm wide angle, 50mm standard, 105mm macro and 300mm telephoto. Extension tubes, three flash units and cables were the main accessories and every picture was taken using a substantial tripod.

Wildlife photography is more to do with understanding the subject than equipment, and making use of that knowledge to get in close or encouraging the subject to behave in the way you want. Almost all the bird photographs were taken using a hide and small subjects such as insects or mice were photographed in my studio.

Finding some subjects is one of the most time-consuming occupations, and working on private land is a real bonus. As a result I am extremely grateful to the many farmers and land-owners who generously allowed me access to their property. I lost count of how many private gardens I visited for the 'garden' book, and I am so appreciative of the welcome and help I received from people who share my interest in natural history. It is always encouraging when someone else shares your enthusiasm for a project, and I am grateful to C.J. Wildbird Foods Ltd. for providing me with a supply of food to tempt everything from blue tits to badgers, woodpeckers to wood mice.

I also wish to thank the whole team of Lion Publishing who have been not only professional and efficient in their approach but also enthusiastic, which makes them a pleasure to work with.

During the two years I spent working on this set of books I needed to spend many days away from home and usually worked very long hours. Throughout, my wife Janet was always encouraging, sharing my failures and frustration as well as my success and without her support it would have been impossible. To say that I am grateful seems inadequate.

Text and pictures copyright © 1996 David Boag

This edition copyright © 1996 Lion Publishing

The author asserts the moral right to be identified as the author of this work

Published by
Lion Publishing plc
Sandy Lane West, Oxford, England
ISBN 0 7459 3174 X
Albatross Books Pty Ltd
PO Box 320, Sutherland, NSW 2232, Australia
ISBN 0 7324 0878 4

First edition 1996

10 9 8 7 6 5 4 3 2 1 0

All rights reserved

A catalogue record for this book is available from the British Library

Printed and bound in the United Arab Emirates

95